how to tell a man by his shoes

Written and illustrated by Kathryn Eisman

**Andrews McMeel
Publishing**

Kansas City

How to Tell a Man by His Shoes

02 03 04 05 06 BID 10 9 8 7 6 5 4 3 2 1

ISBN: 0-7407-2692-7

Library of Congress Control Number: 2002103674

Book design by Holly Camerlinck

To my wonderful parents, Sylvia and Peter Eisman,
for their tremendous sense of humor
and their infinite love and support

A special thank-you to the people who have sprinkled their magic over
my life: Nana Anna Reich, Marcus Einfeld, Jacqui Kraus, Daniel Eisman,
and the extraordinary Siimon Reynolds.

Thanks also my superstar literary agent, Al Zuckerman,
and my editor, Chris Schillig, for helping this young shoe-addict
share her passion with the world.

Contents

Introduction vii
Thong Man 2
Wing-Tip Man 4
Boat Shoe Man 6
Converse All Star Man 8
Snakeskin Cowboy Boot Man 10
Hundred-Dollar Running Shoe Man 12
Monkstrap Man 14
Jesus Sandal Man 16
Gucci Shoe Man 18
Punk Boot Man 20
Tennis Shoe Man 22
Polished Boot Man 24

Clog Man 26
Colorful Hush Puppies Man 28
Reef Sandal Man 30
Italian Loafer Man 32
Doc Martens Man 34
Moccasin Man 36
Motorcycle Boot Man 38
Bowling Shoe Man 40
Yellow Suede Hiking Boot Man 42
Saddle Shoe Man 44
Massage Sandal Man 46
Leather Slide Man 48
Patent Leather Man 50
Platform Shoe Man 52
Barefoot Man 54

Introduction

Finding Mr. Right is becoming increasingly difficult. While women have their tastes, style, and personalities on show for all the world to see in the clothes they wear, men have been protected by the cloak and mask of unified dress regulations, such as the suit and tie. Even in this age of "casual Fridays," the range of male sartorial style is about as wide as the heel of a Manolo Blahnik stiletto. As a result, it is almost impossible to detect any telltale signs about a man's character, until it is too late.

A man's shoes remain one of the few items of apparel through which he exerts any freedom of expression. *His sole is a window into his soul.*

Shoes are unparalleled in their ability to reveal the personality of the wearer. They clearly signify who and what their wearer is, and why he is different from the rest of mankind.

Just as the red heels worn by Louis XIV bespoke nobility, so modern styles whisper the wearer's level of wealth, privilege, class, and character.

This book will be your guide to understanding men from the ground up. With practice, you will learn to instantly identify *your* Mr. Right. You will also gain an insight into the type of man you are dealing with in any situation, be he father, sibling, lover, colleague, or boss.

While no two wearers of the same shoe are identical, you will see a pattern develop, a "type" emerge.

I hope you enjoy your journey through the world of men's shoes, and remember: *if the shoe fits . . .*

how to tell a man by his shoes

Thong Man

Both rogue and sweetheart. Whether he's truly a bum or simply pretending is irrelevant—he looks the part. You'll usually find him stretching the definition of happy hour at the local dive, surrounded by his fun-loving, free-toed friends. He's the one ogling and howling from across the street as your skirt blows up in the breeze. Don't be fooled by this overwhelmingly crude facade—beneath it lurks a gentle, wounded soul. Thong Man secretly longs to share his life with a woman who has a thing for diamonds in the rough. Some of these men welcome polishing, while others fiercely resist; all are hard work.

Pros:

You'll always know where he's going by the flip-flop of his thongs.

Cons:

It will always be the local bar.

Wing-Tip Man

Watch out, ladies: this man means business. He's a professional—JD, MBA, CEO—or maybe all three. He's worked hard to get where he is and demands that those around him work hard, too. He is used to getting what he wants, and while he is a skilled and compelling debater, his "people skills" could use a little work. He likes his women ultrafeminine, with all the softness and gentleness he sometimes lacks. After a long day of competition, he wants his home to be a relaxed haven. In return, he will provide for and protect his woman. Don't try to change this man; he is very set in his ways. At most you'll soften him.

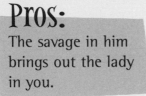

Pros:
The savage in him
brings out the lady
in you.

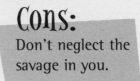

Cons:
Don't neglect the
savage in you.

Boat Shoe Man

Classically handsome, relaxed, elegant, and sophisticated (the shoe, that is). Perfect for those Sunday brunches on his boat. This man values good craftsmanship above all else and is loyal to things he considers to be of a high quality. He isn't a huge fan of change (after all, it's been a long, *long* time since devotees of the preppy look made the Sperry Top-Sider the shoe of the moment), yet he's the first to embark on an adventure. The juxtaposition of security and excitement can make this man a great partner. He is very sociable and enjoys spending quality time with family and friends, preferably outdoors, free from the cares of the office. A romantic weekend away wouldn't be out of the question—so ask! His ideal woman is naturally elegant and a great hostess.

Pros:

You'll feel like you're sailing through a Nautica ad whenever you're together.

Cons:

All waves crash. Keep your wits about you.

Converse All Star Man

Classic slacker cool. These old school kicks were the Air Jordans of their time. But it's been a long time since "Chucks" ruled the hard court, and these days they stand for anything *but* rigorous athletic effort. Today's All Star Dude cultivates a decidedly laid-back approach to life. Generally a few days out from his last shave, he isn't usually classically handsome, yet remains intriguing. All Star Man is often highly skilled in an "outsider" sport such as skating, surfing, snowboarding, or even acting. He is happiest pursuing his own interests and is quite content to go against the grain. His mind is very active, and his thoughts may be in the stars when you converse. A woman would need to be both daring and sexy to attract his attention. Buy yourself some sexy panties and make him eggs on white toast while wearing them and little else. It will blow his mind.

Pros:

He's genuinely old school cool.

Cons:

If you appreciate that he's old school cool, you're probably new school cool—and that's a clash.

Snakeskin Cowboy Boot Man

This guy has a story to tell, but you're probably not interested in hearing it. He might buy you a drink and confess to finding you irresistible. You might find yourself vacillating between laughing with him and at him. You might even be charmed by his lame come-ons and poorly masked vulnerability. And there is something ridiculously sexual about his humorous, even distasteful groin-led stance, something undeniably dirty and raunchy. It's sexy to watch yourself turn him on, even if you don't want to. Let him buy you a drink; perhaps listen to a story or two, if only for a laugh. This guy is really just a bit of fun under all that skin. He needs a girl who's confident enough to hear his corny lines and silly enough to blush.

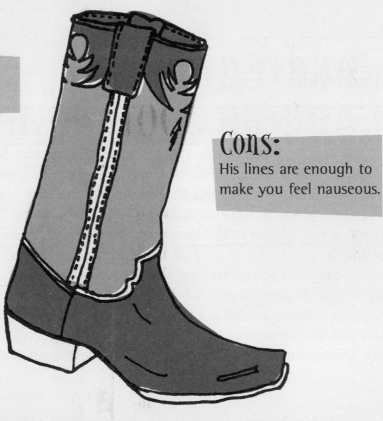

Pros:
He makes you
feel naughty.

Cons:
His lines are enough to
make you feel nauseous.

Hundred-Dollar Running Shoe Man

This man is educated in the benefits of exercise, but sometimes going for a jog is just too much hard work. Although he is ambitious and driven in all aspects of his life, he is constantly fighting his lazy side. Having the best running shoes doesn't make you go for a run, but he hopes it might help. This man may seek too much pleasure through the acquisition of wealth and conspicuous consumption; never wanting to be outdone, Hundred-Dollar Running Shoe Man often places himself under enormous pressure. His competitive streak means that in order to appreciate his woman, he needs to believe that she's the best, and that he is lucky to have won her. She must be independent, self-assured, and dedicated to her career.

Pros:
Despite his apparent slackness, he's actually highly motivated.

Cons:
His occasional bouts of selfishness can leave you unexpectedly out of the picture.

Monkstrap Man

As he walks up to you with a pseudosmooth grin on his face, you may wonder if he's trying to sell you a car. Smile back and know that his car salesman's persona is only a role he believes he's meant to play—thank God he hasn't mastered it yet. Ask him about his favorite album, because he's passionate about music. Tell him a joke, as he loves a good laugh, and it will help you both relax. Let him take you to an inexpensive local restaurant for dinner. Later in the relationship he may want to treat himself (and you) to a romantic night at a luxury hotel. If you don't intimidate this guy, he's likely to reveal his soft and caring side.

Pros:

He's a much better boyfriend than he looks like he would be.

Cons:

He may slip back into that pseudosmooth person every so often; just sit it out.

Jesus Sandal Man

The shoe of the dreamer, the hopeless romantic. There is a soulfulness and gentleness to this man that women find magnetic, leather straps aside. Whether he is on an exotic holiday or planning one in his head, this man has a nomadic core—cocooned from external trends, enslaved by his inner passion. Together you'll discover another world, a hidden oasis by the beach or a secluded treehouse in the hills. He is in search of the nymphet, a fallen angel with a broken spirit for him to mend.

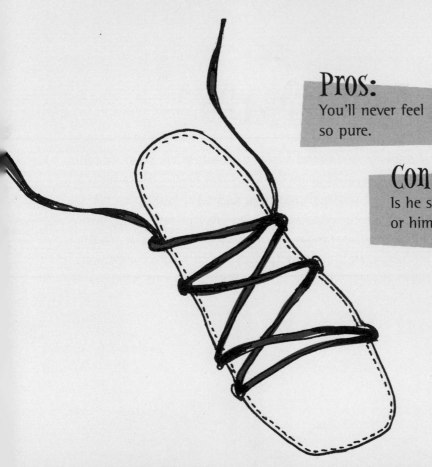

Pros:
You'll never feel
so pure.

Cons:
Is he saving you
or himself?

Gucci Shoe Man

He's so slick. He's either a star or on his way through the solar system. He enjoys luxury and believes that he deserves the best. The same is true for his women. They must be well groomed, as he finds ill-groomed women intolerable. He appreciates comfort but would sacrifice it for glamour. He could be anything from an up-and-coming lawyer to an up-and-coming designer. He's either your boss or not so secretly planning to be. This man craves excitement, and he's willing to work for it.

Pros:
Expect the latest designer handbag each season.

Cons:
Remember that "handbags" only last a season.

Punk Boot Man

You'll know whether this punk's the real McCoy when you ask him to recite the words to every Sex Pistols song. If he can, this guy is sure to have attitude to boot—staring intensely from under pierced brows, swaying past you on a city street, contentedly uneasy in his skin-tight jeans. Punk Boot Man believes he's a social commentator, even a revolutionary. A natural loner, he does not seek close relationships; his inner demons are keeping him company. If he can focus his enormous energy and passion on a worthy cause, he has the potential to be a great leader. If not, he risks leading a life plagued with frustration. Naturally drawn to the excitement of a subculture, he is likely to work in the underbelly of society (perhaps as a writer for an underground newspaper or an offbeat web-site designer). His woman, too, must be independent, genuinely unafraid of being alone, and equally antiestablishment.

Pros:
His ideas may alter the way you perceive society.

Cons:
Don't let him put *his* chip on *your* shoulder.

Tennis Shoe Man

He is genuinely competent, and much of that is due to his organizational skills. Tennis Shoe Man's motto in life is "You can't always be the most intelligent, but you can always be the most prepared." This white-soled player likes rules, and his perfect love match will abide by the laws set. He finds strength in predicting other people's actions and forecasting emerging trends. As a result, he fears irrational and illogical partners. Tennis Shoe Man is family-oriented and exceptionally loyal; get him in your corner and he'll serve you well.

Pros:
If you like systems and order, this could be love.

Cons:
He's a bit of a traditionalist, so make sure you don't end up doing all the serving.

Polished Boot Man

Seriously sharp. You may find yourself taken aback by this man's intense ambition. He is suave and sophisticated. This guy knows how to live alone and likes the ring of the title "bachelor." Indeed, he has made serious progress by himself and now cherishes freedom as if it were success. He's friendly and polite but can easily become distant and aloof. You're only ever half sure he's interested in you. This man revels in stimulating, analytical conversation, yet never gives too much of himself away. If you're not intimidated by his confidence, you might notice that he's working you with every word. Play it cool, girl. Stop biting your nails, stop flipping your hair, and stop mouthing off! Instead, ask yourself, "Is he good enough for me?" The answer is probably yes, but he doesn't have to know that.

Pros:
Witty repartee.

Cons:
Remember, you're
half of that
clever conversation.

Clog Man

Clog Man dances to his own beat, all the while clumping his clunky feet. Perhaps he is indeed cool, perhaps he's such a pioneer that we cannot yet fathom his brilliance, or perhaps he's such a smug dork that he cannot recognize his own poor judgment. But say this for Clog Man: no one who's heard him clip-clopping down the street like a wayward Budweiser Clydesdale can deny that he has guts. Clog Man has a strange and difficult past, and his future looks to be following that same trend—but it would be the only thing about Clog Man that is following a trend. He is a questionable character indeed, one who wears his broken heart on his ripped sleeve. But do not write off Cloggy just yet. Let him lurk awhile longer, and you will discover a chasm full of intriguing facts that make this man different from any other you've met. And for the innovation and eccentricity he brings to your world, you will be grateful.

Pros:
He will show you that normality is false.

Cons:
And in the process prove that insanity is real.

Colorful Hush Puppies Man

Perhaps these were what the King was harping on when he sang about his blue suede shoes—but then again, Hush Puppies have always been a little more Pat Boone than Elvis. Colorful Hush Puppies Man's clean-cut take on risqué is a welcome change in our jaded world. He is an adventurous little puppy who doesn't like being on a tight leash. Irrespective of whether he's been a naughty boy or not, his enthusiasm for life and his seemingly incorruptible naïveté will leave you panting. For he is still enchanted by the world, and how enchanting is that?

Pros:
Finally, someone
to take you
out dancing.

Cons:
He's on his own
adventure,
so don't get
too close.

Reef Sandal Man

Rough and ready. His large tanned toes have run Class IV rapids on the Snake River and hiked the Himalayan trails. Reef Sandal Man dreams of living in India, Africa, or Nepal. He's used to being alone, and he's proud of being able to be. Fiercely independent and impossible to tie down, this adrenaline junkie essentially aches for a companion. Reef Sandal Man seeks a soul mate with whom he can explore the world, a Lola Granola with a spiritual connection to the land and an insatiable sense of adventure.

Pros:

You'll experience people and places you'd otherwise only dream of.

Cons:

Good luck trying to persuade him to settle down; get used to carrying a backpack.

Italian Loafer Man

Naturally stylish. This man has a high regard for sensual pleasures—good wine, good food, and good-looking women. He appreciates relaxed glamour (an Italian white by the pool) and dreams of being draped in fresh linen and supple flesh. He seeks a poised serenity in his lady. Italian Loafer Man needs a woman who can move effortlessly between being passionate and aloof. His lady must also be capable of turning on the charm and wit when necessary.

Pros:
Dining out at lots of wonderful restaurants.

Cons:
His genuine appreciation of all things beautiful may test his fidelity and your strength.

Doc Martens Man

A decade ago, the Docs devil stomped and slammed his way through the clubs of London on the feet of punks, skins, and mods. They were later corrupted by every wanna-be cultivating the downtown art director by day/anarchist by night look. Alas, the glory days are over, and the modern Docs dude can't put a foot right. His taste in women reflects that of his shoes, sturdy and no-frills. He may fantasize about the glamazon, but in life the comfortable, faithful types are a better fit. Beware of the man who has tried to dress up his shoes by coloring in the yellow stitching around the sole. He's accomplished at covering things up—like the fact that he's too cheap to buy proper dress shoes.

Pros:
With a reliable income, he'll never quit his job.

Cons:
It would be more exciting getting an enema.

Moccasin Man

Simplicity is the key here, as he values quality over trends. This man possesses a relaxed elegance that is timeless and alluring. While Moccasin Man may be average looking, he always seems to have a beautiful woman by his side (sometimes both sides). This phenomenon often baffles other men, but the explanation is simple: he appears completely comfortable in his own skin, and this confidence is unequivocally appealing to beautiful, often excessively self-aware women. Moccasin Man appreciates a chic woman, so pull out your breeziest white linen dress, spend the extra twenty minutes needed to ensure that your makeup looks totally natural, and practice revealing your effortless grace.

Pros:
His confidence means you can relax.

Cons:
Just because he thinks he's perfect doesn't make it so.

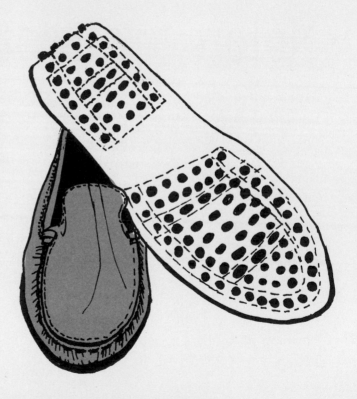

Motorcycle Boot Man

Expect a departure from life as you know it when you enter the uncharted world of Motorcycle Boot Man. His dark, dangerous, impetuous veneer will lure you in, but you'll stay searching for the sensitive essence he only occasionally reveals. Don't be hurt if he pulls back each time you connect. Motorcycle Boot Man is not used to being vulnerable; in fact, it is the thing he most fears. Watch as he moonlights between man and child. He needs to be subtly nurtured by a woman; anything more will scare him off. Trust that while he may never admit it, he knows he'd be lost without his lover. But don't forget that feeling lost is an emotion he's quite comfortable with. This urban cowboy can be startlingly selfish and unreliable; if he's with you, it's because he genuinely wants to be. While Motorcycle Boot Man does know the meaning of loyalty, etiquette is a concept he has yet to grasp.

Pros:
He'll teach you
to be strong.

Cons:
Think about what
that means.

Bowling Shoe Man

Quite different from the average Joe knocking down pins and pints on league night at his local bowling alley, the man wearing these babies on the street is aching to distinguish himself from the masses. Bowling Shoe Boy has worked hard to develop his innovative style and may fiercely refuse to correct anything you might see as a "character flaw," instead regarding it as a "lovable idiosyncrasy." His need to stand out from the crowd may become tiresome as you realize that by purposely opposing the masses, he is more strongly influenced by them. A huge movie buff and often a collector of arcane memorabilia, this man is fascinated by the obscure or the rare. Buy him an original retro anything or cultivate an unusual interpretation of a cult film, and he's yours.

Pros:
A man with initiative
and original ideas.

Cons:
A little subtlety
wouldn't hurt.

Yellow Suede Hiking Boot Man

Hiking boot? Yes. Rugged? I'm not so sure. A remnant from a main-stream fashion trend, these boots are most often favored by the type of suburban warrior who drives his SUV to pick up his kids from school. By wearing such unnecessarily robust footwear, Yellow Suede Hiking Boot Man is subconsciously clinging to a masculinity dissolved by modern-day domesticity. Sure, he fantasizes about a hearty hike up the nearest 14,000-foot mountain, but there are more important things to do at home and at work. Humor this man's frustrated ego. Make him feel like the hunter and protector, and he'll love you forever.

Pros:
He wants to have
a more adventurous life.

Cons:
He's wanted a more
adventurous life all
his life.

Saddle Shoe Man

This gentleman exhibits great style and panache. Aware of the power of appearances, he takes pride in the image he portrays. The older he is, the more protective he is by nature. A senior Saddle Shoe Man will insist that you never carry anything heavier than a flower and will refuse to discuss unpleasant topics in a lady's presence, to avoid polluting "female innocence." The junior Saddle Shoe Man is quirky and imaginative. He likes to play around with tradition, and while he appreciates Old World glamour, he does not take precedents too seriously. In this way, he is an unusual breed of neo-nonconformist, embracing the past while gently mocking it. Enjoy this man's lateral thinking and creative lovemaking.

Pros:
Old World meets New Age.

Cons:
His quirkiness can appear a tad studied.

Massage Sandal Man

It's little wonder that this man needs a massage; anyone would, after spending the day on those spikes. Next they'll invent the therapeutic hot-coal insole. To spare himself a bit of pain, the Massage Sandal Masochist may commit an even more heinous "fashion don't" by donning his sandals with a pair of socks. However distasteful these shoes look, one must acknowledge and even admire this man's flagrant disregard for aesthetics and his utter ignorance of style. Whether or not you'll ever feel comfortable with his looks is irrelevant; it is apparent that this man is comfortable with himself. And there *is* something alluring about that. He seeks a tolerant and practical woman, a lady who considers Friday night happy hour the highlight of the week. He needs a woman with whom he can share the beauty, burdens, and bunions of life.

Pros:
He knows who he is
and isn't afraid of being himself.

Cons:
This relationship could
be sole destroying (literally).

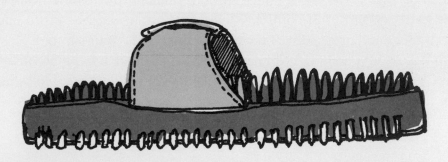

Leather Slide Man

"Everyone look, I'm relaxed!" Leather Slide Man prides himself on living the good life. He desires nothing more than a late Sunday afternoon cocktail with his friends and their girlfriends. He's very body-conscious and probably works out. Slides add the finishing touch to his "athlete at rest" look. Leather Slide Man wants an easygoing, equally body-conscious girlfriend who has a bunch of good-looking friends. He despises being stressed or out of control. To combat this, he works hard to have it "all together," or at least appear to. Leather Slide Man can be painfully aloof when he feels smothered. Keep things breezy, because there is nothing more infuriating than being told to "calm down" when you are not being HYSTERICAL!

Pros:

Lots of mango daiquiris and a great tan.

Cons:

Is being this relaxed downright stressful?

Patent Leather Man

If tackiness were an idea, this man would have it patented. His shoes are shinier than his boss's shoes, indeed shinier than a space station solar panel. He is an outgoing man—yes, an extrovert. But if you look a little deeper, you will discover a thinker, a dreamer. Patent Leather Pal is both performer and audience. He is an optimist unafraid of taking chances, a man desperate to bring romance back into everyday life. It is this desperation, this optimism, that is at the root of both his greatest successes and his biggest failures, as he often looks too eager to be taken seriously. To entice this knight in shining footwear, think flashy and trashy. Leave your good taste at the door and celebrate your new-found freedom by drinking designer martinis and dancing the night away in a gold Lurex dress. (But wear something nice underneath, too. He'll be able to see everything in the reflection off his high-gloss shoes.)

Pros:
Glamour isn't dead.

Cons:
Neither is bad taste.

Platform Shoe Man

Platform Shoe Man is desperately clinging to his masculinity. If his ego were in the driver's seat, a blond hottie would be in the back. Platform Shoe Man is sexually ravenous and eager to prove that he can rise to any occasion (even if it requires a little help). Being a feisty contender and a hardworking lover, this man doesn't get much time to relax. Even if he seems to be doing nothing, you can be sure that his inner turbines are refueling for the next onslaught. Platform Shoe Pal has many secret insecurities, all of which he has taken great pains to hide, often by overachieving. He wants the beautiful, popular girl he could never date at school. Be the "fantasy" girl for him to look up to, and maybe he'll stop awhile to enjoy what he's been working so hard for.

Pros:
Lethargy and purposelessness will be vanquished forever.

Cons:
Does he really love you, or are you just another platform to climb?

Barefoot Man

Endless possibilities. He is the splendid male specimen who resides under the surface of every man. Barefoot Man is refreshingly relaxed in his own skin. He is perfectly at peace with himself, even though that may mean he does some things that nauseate you. He represents the quintessential primal beast. He is simple in his desires, seeking food (steak and potatoes), water (a.k.a. beer), shelter (with a comfy couch), and, of course, procreation (or at least practice for it). Only when these goals have been achieved is he truly content. To win his heart, just satisfy these needs: greet him with a kiss and a smile after work, cook his favorite meal, let him relax on the couch, and entice him into ravishing you in the bedroom. He is loyal and protective of those he truly loves. Be aware that he has little control over his urges; he is a hunter, not a gatherer.

Pros:
He is pure man.

Cons:
He is pure man.

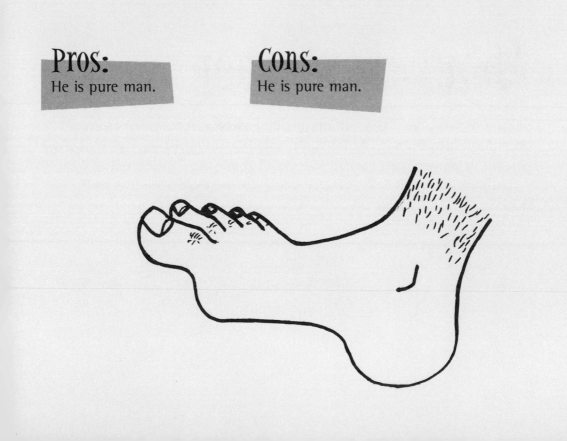

About the Author

Kathryn Eisman has drawn on her lifelong passion for shoes as the inspiration for this, her first book. An exciting young writer, she is also a communications student and a successful model.

Kathryn lives in Sydney, Australia, just up the road from five shoe stores.